OK

It's a book all about YOU!
It asks you hundreds of questions
about yourself and provides you
with spaces to fill in the answers.
Write the answers in pencil just in
case you make a mistake, then
you can rub out what you've written
and start again. Once you have
completed the book it will be a
unique guide to everything there is
to know about you. There has never
been a book quite like this one
before – and that's simply because
there isn't anyone in the world
quite like *you*.

ME!

My name is ....

My address is ....

My telephone number is ....

My age is ....

The name of my school is ....

My form is ....

Colour of hair ....

Colour of eyes ....

Distinguishing marks ....

Height ....

Weight ....

ME!

*(Stick a photograph
of yourself here.)*

Illustrated by
Rowan Barnes-Murphy
and . . . .
(Fill in your name here.)

KNIGHT BOOKS
HODDER AND STOUGHTON

Printed and bound in Great Britain for
Hodder and Stoughton Paperbacks, a
division of Hodder and Stoughton Ltd.,
Mill Road, Dunton Green, Sevenoaks,
Kent (Editorial Office: 47 Bedford
Square, London, WC1 3DP) by
Hunt Barnard Printing Ltd.,
Aylesbury, Bucks.

ISBN 0 340 24027 X

CONTENTS

MY NAME

MY FIRST NAME IS: _Alaina_

MY OTHER FORENAMES ARE: _Claire_

_____

(All the names that come before your surname
are your 'forenames', so if you are called John
Julian James Jones, put Julian James here.)

MY SURNAME IS: _Michie_

I MIGHT HAVE BEEN CALLED: _____
(Ask your parents what other names they were
thinking of giving you before they decided to call
you what they did.)

IF I HAD BEEN A MEMBER OF THE OPPOSITE SEX, I MIGHT HAVE BEEN CALLED:

Andrew alexsander Michie

(If you're a boy, ask your parents what they would have called you if you had been a girl. And if you're a girl, ask your parents what they would have called you if you had been a boy.)

MY NICKNAME IS: _Ally_

IF I COULD HAVE A DIFFERENT FIRST NAME, THIS IS THE ONE I WOULD CHOOSE:

Sharon

(If you're called Susan and you'd rather be called Victoria, write Victoria here – and if you're called Victoria and you'd rather be called Susan, write Susan here!)

IF I COULD HAVE A DIFFERENT SURNAME, THIS IS THE ONE I WOULD CHOOSE:

Michie

(If you have rather an ordinary surname, choosing an unusual new one can be fun. There is a man in San Francisco who has changed his name to Vladimir Zzzzzzabakov in order to make sure that his is the last name in the telephone directory!)

IF I COULD HAVE A PEN-NAME, THIS IS THE ONE I WOULD CHOOSE:

_____

2

(The pen name of Charles Dodgson was Lewis Carroll. The pen name of Samuel Clemens was Mark Twain. If you were a writer, what would your pen name be?)

MY FIRST NAME MEANS: _____

_____

(Most first names have a special meaning and all first names have a history. At the library find a book about first names and look yours up to find out what it means.)

MY SURNAME MEANS: _____

_____

(If your surname is Butcher or Baker or Farmer it's obvious what it means, but if it is a more unusual name you will have to find a Dictionary of Surnames and look it up.)

MY FAVOURITE NAMESAKE IS:_____

_____

(Someone who has the same name as you is called your namesake. Of all the people in the world who share either your first name or your surname who do you admire most?)

MY BIRTH

I WAS BORN AT: _____
(Give the exact hour and minute when you were born.)

ON:_____
(Give the day of the week, the date and the month when you were born.)

IN: _____
(Give the year when you were born.)

THIS IS WHERE I WAS BORN:

_____

_____

(Give the name and address of the hospital or
place where you were born.)

THESE ARE THE PEOPLE WHO WERE PRESENT WHEN I
WAS BORN:

_____

_____

(Give the names of the doctors, midwives and
nurses who were there when you were born.)

WHEN I WAS BORN I WEIGHED: _____
(Like almost all the information needed for this
page, to find this out you will have to check with
your mother.)

I SHARE MY BIRTHDAY WITH: _My Preinds_

_____

(If you were born on 24 May you share your
birthday with Queen Victoria. If you were born
on 14 March you share your birthday with Albert
Einstein. If you were born on 23 April you share
your birthday with William Shakespeare. If you
were born on Christmas Day you share your
birthday with Sir Isaac Newton. Find out if you
share your birthday with anyone famous.)

5

MY STAR SIGN

MY STAR SIGN IS: _Leo the lion_

MY BIRTHSTONE IS: _Sardonyx_

MY FLOWER IS: _gladiolus_

MY COLOUR IS: _orange_

MY LUCKY NUMBER IS: _one_

MY LUCKY DAY IS: _Monday_

(Your Star Sign, Birthstone, Flower, Colour, Lucky Number and Lucky Day all depend on when you were born.)

THE SIGN OF ARIES, THE RAM
for those born between 22 March and 20 April
Birthstone: Diamond
Flower: Daisy
Colour: Red
Lucky Number: 3
Lucky Day: Thursday

THE SIGN OF TAURUS, THE BULL
for those born between 21 April and 21 May
Birthstone: Emerald
Flower: Lily-of-the-valley
Colour: Yellow
Lucky Number: 10
Lucky Day: Sunday

THE SIGN OF GEMINI, THE TWINS
for those born between 22 May and 22 June
Birthstone: Pearl
Flower: Rose
Colour: Violet
Lucky Number: 7
Lucky Day: Friday

THE SIGN OF CANCER, THE CRAB
for those born between 23 June and 23 July
Birthstone: Ruby
Flower: Water lily
Colour: Green
Lucky Number: 5
Lucky Day: Wednesday

THE SIGN OF LEO, THE LION
for those born between 24 July and 23 August
Birthstone: Sardonyx
Flower: Gladiolus
Colour: Orange
Lucky Number: 1
Lucky Day: Monday

THE SIGN OF VIRGO, THE VIRGIN
for those born between 24 August and
23 September
Birthstone: Sapphire
Flower: Carnation
Colour: Violet
Lucky Number: 2
Lucky Day: Saturday

THE SIGN OF LIBRA, THE SCALES
for those born between 24 September and
23 October
Birthstone: Opal
Flower: Marigold
Colour: Yellow
Lucky Number: 4
Lucky Day: Tuesday

THE SIGN OF SCORPIO, THE SCORPION
for those born between 24 October and
22 November
Birthstone: Topaz
Flower: Chrysanthemum
Colour: Red
Lucky Number: 8
Lucky Day: Friday

THE SIGN OF SAGITTARIUS, THE ARCHER

for those born between 23 November and
22 December
Birthstone: Turquoise
Flower: Narcissus
Colour: Purple
Lucky Number: 5
Lucky Day: Tuesday

THE SIGN OF CAPRICORN, THE GOAT

for those born between 23 December and
19 January
Birthstone: Garnet
Flower: Tulip
Colour: Deep blue
Lucky Number: 8
Lucky Day: Sunday

THE SIGN OF AQUARIUS, THE WATER CARRIER

for those born between 20 January and
19 February
Birthstone: Amethyst
Flower: Violet

Colour: Light blue
Lucky Number: 11
Lucky Day: Monday

THE SIGN OF PISCES, THE FISH
for those born between 20 February and
21 March
Birthstone: Bloodstone
Flower: Daffodil
Colour: Gold
Lucky Number: 10
Lucky Day: Wednesday

MY BODY

MY HEIGHT IS: _____

MY WEIGHT IS: _____

THE COLOUR OF MY HAIR IS: _____

THE COLOUR OF MY EYES IS: _____

I HAVE TO WEAR SPECTACLES: _____(Yes or No)

I AM LEFT-HANDED: _____(Yes or No)

THE LENGTH OF MY LEFT ARM IS: _____

THE LENGTH OF MY RIGHT ARM IS: _____
(Measure your arms with a tape measure from the shoulder to the tip of your longest finger. You might expect both arms to be exactly the same length, but you will be surprised to find that one of them is almost certainly a fraction longer than the other.)

THE LENGTH OF MY LEFT LEG IS:_____

THE LENGTH OF MY RIGHT LEG IS:_____
(Measure from your hip bone down to the ground.)

THE LENGTH OF MY LEFT FOOT IS: _____

THE LENGTH OF MY RIGHT FOOT IS: _____
(Measure along the bottom of your foot, from the heel to the tip of your longest toe.)

11

HEIGHT AND WEIGHT CHART

(Use this chart to see how your weight and height change as you grow older. Weigh and measure yourself every three months. Mark your height in one colour and your weight in another.)

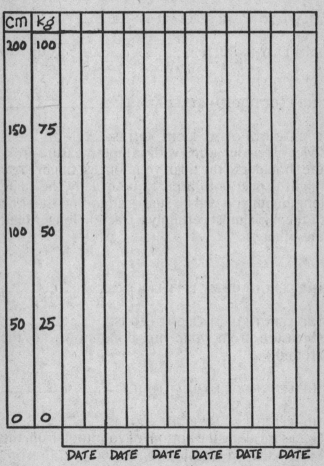

MY PHYSICAL PECULIARITIES ARE:

_____

_____

_____

(Don't worry if you haven't got any! But if you happen to have an interesting birthmark on your body or a scar or any other physical feature that's a bit out of the ordinary, this is the place to record it.)

MY HEART BEAT IS: _____
(To find out how fast your heart beats you will need to take your pulse. To take your own pulse place a finger on your wrist just here:

If you have your finger in the right place you'll feel a steady beat. Take a watch with a second hand and count the number of beats in sixty seconds. Your heart beat depends on how old you are: it slows down as you grow older. A baby has a heart that beats 130 times a minute, but the average adult has a heart that only beats 70 times a minute.)

MY BREATHING RATE IS: _____
(Count the number of times you breathe in and out in sixty seconds. The average person sitting normally reading this book will breathe between ten and fourteen times in one minute.)

Illness
(You will need to get this information either from your mother or from your doctor when you next visit him. Don't make a note of every time you went to bed with a heavy cold! Just record all the serious illnesses you have ever had – measles, mumps, chicken pox, etc. – with the date and the number of days you stayed in bed.)

14

ILLNESS   DATE   NO. OF DAYS IN BED

Hospital
(If ever you have been a hospital patient, put the date when you were in hospital, the reason why you were in hospital and the name of the hospital here.)

DATE:_____

REASON:_____

HOSPITAL: _____

_____

MY FINGERPRINTS

My right hand

My left hand

MY FAMILY

MY MOTHER   MY FATHER

FIRST NAME:

SURNAME:

MAIDEN NAME:

COLOUR OF EYES:

COLOUR OF HAIR:

OCCUPATION:

THE MOST IMPORTANT
 DAY OF THEIR LIFE
 SO FAR:

WHAT THEY WANT
 MOST:

MY BROTHERS AND SISTERS

(If you haven't got any brothers and sisters, you can always *invent* some! Pretend that you have a brother or a sister and write in imaginary information about them.)

FIRST NAME:

SURNAME:

DATE OF BIRTH:

PLACE OF BIRTH:

ADDRESS:

TELEPHONE NUMBER:

HEIGHT:

WEIGHT:

COLOUR OF EYES:

COLOUR OF HAIR:

THE MOST IMPORTANT
 DAY OF THEIR LIFE
 SO FAR:

WHAT THEY WANT
 MOST:

MY AUNTS

(Your aunts are the sisters of your parents or the wives of the brothers of your parents.)

NAME   SISTER OR WIFE OF

MY UNCLES

(Your uncles are the brothers of your parents or the husbands of the sisters of your parents.)

NAME   BROTHER OR HUSBAND OF

MY FIRST COUSINS

(If any of your uncles or aunts have children, they are your first cousins.)

NAME   CHILDREN OF

Catherine is brilliant!

MY FAMILY MOTTO IS: _____

_____

(If you don't have a Family Motto – and most families don't – invent one!)

MY FAMILY COAT OF ARMS LOOKS LIKE THIS:
(If you don't have a Family Coat of Arms – and most families don't – design one.)

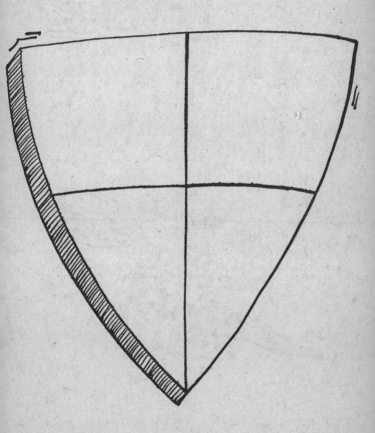

Pet No. 1 Pet No. 2 Pet No. 3

NAME OF PET: hazel

BREED OR SPECIES
OF PET: Rabbit

COLOUR OF PET: grey orange brown

HEIGHT OF PET:

WEIGHT OF PET:

AGE OF PET:

PET'S FAVOURITE
FOOD: cabage

PET'S FAVOURITE
DRINK: Water

PET'S SPECIAL TRICKS:

THE PET I'D MOST LIKE TO OWN IS:

_____

(If you don't own a pet, put the name of the pet you would like to have. If you already have a pet, put the name of a different kind of pet.)

IF I COULD HAVE A WILD ANIMAL AS A PET, THIS IS THE ANIMAL I WOULD CHOOSE:

_____

THE ANIMAL I LIKE BEST IN THE WORLD IS:

_____

THE ANIMAL I LIKE LEAST IN THE WORLD IS:

_____

THE BIRD I LIKE BEST IN THE WORLD IS:

_____

THE BIRD I LIKE LEAST IN THE WORLD IS:

_____

MY FAVOURITE 'MADE-UP' ANIMAL IS:

_____

(Writers, cartoonists, film-makers have invented hundreds of different animals – Snoopy, Mickey Mouse, Winnie the Pooh, Paddington Bear, Basil Brush, Peter Rabbit, etc. – and of all the made-up animals you have heard of, which one is your favourite?)

MY FRIENDS

(As well as listing the names, addresses and birthdays of your ten closest friends, give each one of them a mark out of 10. Your best friend will score 10 out of 10.

NAME	NICKNAME	ADDRESS
1. Lisa	Lis	30 Sedge Fieldclose
2.		
3.		
4.		
5.		
6.		
7.		
8.		
9.		
10.		

26

The friends you like a lot will score 7, 8 and 9.
The friends you don't like so much will score a
little less. Any one who only scores 1 or 2
shouldn't really be on the list at all!)

TELEPHONE NUMBER	BIRTHDAY	SCORE OUT OF 10

MY HOME

MY ADDRESS IS:

_____(Name of street

_____or block of flats)

_____(Town)

_____(County)

_____(Postal Code)

_____(Country)

_____(Continent)

MY TELEPHONE NUMBER IS: _____

THE AREA CODE IS: _____

MY HOME IS CALLED: _____
(Most houses and flats just have numbers, but some have names. If you live in a house with a name, write it here.)

MY HOME SHOULD BE CALLED: _____
(Invent a name for your home.)

THIS IS WHAT MY HOME LOOKS LIKE:

(Draw a picture of the outside of the building where you live.)

IN MY HOME THERE ARE _____ROOMS.

MY FAVOURITE ROOM IS: _____

MY LEAST FAVOURITE ROOM IS: _____

30

IN MY HOME THERE ARE _____STAIRS.

IN MY HOME THERE ARE _____WINDOWS.

IN MY HOME THERE ARE _____DOORS.

THIS IS A GROUND PLAN OF MY HOME:

(And if you're not sure of what a ground plan should look like, here's a ground plan of our illustrator's home. Do a separate ground plan for each floor. If you live in a flat or a bungalow or a caravan you will only need one ground plan.)

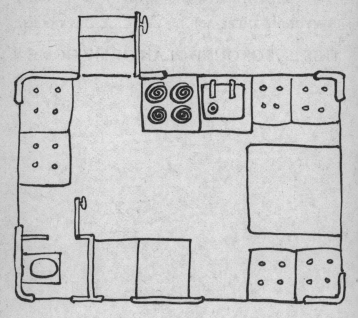

AN INVENTORY OF MY HOME
(Go through each room in your home making an inventory. The inventory will be a record of all the articles and pieces of furniture in the house. Make a note of the number of items here.)

CHAIRS:

TABLES:

ARMCHAIRS:

SOFAS:

BEDS:

CHESTS OF DRAWERS:

CUPBOARDS:

PICTURES:

LIGHTS:

TELEPHONES:

TV SETS:

RADIOS:

RECORD PLAYERS:

TAPE RECORDERS:

CARPETS:

MIRRORS:

ORNAMENTS:

ASHTRAYS:

COOKERS:

REFRIGERATORS:

FREEZERS:

KITCHEN EQUIPMENT:

COOKING UTENSILS:

CROCKERY:

CUTLERY:

SHEETS:

PILLOW CASES:

BLANKETS:

DUVETS:

MATTRESSES:

WASH-BASINS:

BATHS:

LAVATORIES:

WASHING MACHINES:

TUMBLE DRYERS:

VACUUM CLEANERS:

BRUSHES & BROOMS:

34

MY OLD HOMES

THESE ARE THE ADDRESSES OF HOMES THAT I USED TO
LIVE IN, WITH THE DATES THAT I LIVED THERE.
(You will probably have to ask your parents for
this information.)

1. _____ _____

2. _____ _____

3. _____ _____

4. _____ _____

5. _____ _____

MY IDEAL HOME
IF I COULD HAVE ANY HOME AT ALL, THIS IS WHAT IT
WOULD LOOK LIKE:

(Draw a picture of your dream house here.)

MY ROOM IS _____LONG.

MY ROOM IS _____WIDE.

MY ROOM IS _____HIGH.

IF THE WALLS OF MY ROOM COULD BE ANY COLOUR, THIS IS THE COLOUR I WOULD CHOOSE:

_____

IF THE CURTAINS IN MY ROOM COULD BE ANY COLOUR, THIS IS THE COLOUR I WOULD CHOOSE:

_____

IF THE CARPET IN MY ROOM COULD BE ANY COLOUR, THIS IS THE COLOUR I WOULD CHOOSE:

_____

36

THIS IS A GROUND PLAN OF MY ROOM:

MY GARDEN IS_____LONG AND_____WIDE.

THE NUMBER OF TREES IN MY GARDEN: _____

THE NUMBER OF FLOWER BEDS IN MY GARDEN:____

THE NUMBER OF PLANTS IN MY GARDEN: _____

THE NUMBER OF SHRUBS IN MY GARDEN: _____

MY FAVOURITE FLOWER IS:_____

MY FAVOURITE TREE IS: _____

THE NEAREST PARK OR PUBLIC GARDENS TO MY HOME
IS CALLED:

_____

THIS IS A GROUND PLAN OF MY GARDEN:

(If you don't have a garden, draw a plan of the one you would like to have.)

MY NEIGHBOURHOOD

THIS IS A MAP OF MY NEIGHBOURHOOD:

(If you are not sure how to draw a map of your neighbourhood, you can get quite a good idea from this map of our illustrator's neighbourhood.)

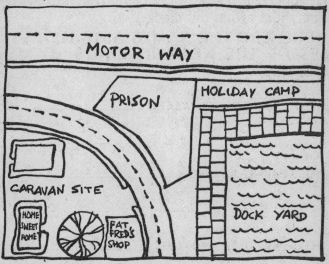

THE NEIGHBOURS I LIKE BEST ARE CALLED:

_____

THEY LIVE AT: _____

_____

THE NEIGHBOURS I LIKE LEAST ARE CALLED:

_____

THEY LIVE AT: _____

_____

IN THE STREET WHERE I LIVE THERE ARE___HOUSES.
(If you live in a block of flats, find out how many
flats there are in the block.)

HERE ARE THE NAMES AND ADDRES-
SES OF THE NEAREST SHOPS TO MY
HOME.

THE NEAREST SUPERMARKET: _____

_____

THE NEAREST BUTCHER: _____

_____

THE NEAREST FISHMONGER: _____

_____

THE NEAREST GREENGROCER: _____

_____

THE NEAREST BAKER: _____

_____

THE NEAREST NEWSAGENT: _____

_____

42

THE NEAREST CHEMIST: _____

_____

THE NEAREST IRONMONGER: _____

_____

THE NEAREST BOOKSHOP: _____

_____

THE NEAREST DEPARTMENT STORE: _____

_____

THE NEAREST CLOTHES SHOP: _____

_____

THE NEAREST SHOE SHOP: _____

_____

THE NEAREST POST OFFICE: _____

_____

THE NEAREST BANK: _____

_____

MY SCHOOL IS: _____

_____

THE ADDRESS OF MY SCHOOL IS: _____

_____

_____

MY SCHOOL WAS FOUNDED IN: _____

THE HEAD TEACHER AT MY SCHOOL IS CALLED:

_____

MY FORM TEACHER IS CALLED: _____

IN MY SCHOOL THERE ARE_____TEACHERS.

MY FAVOURITE TEACHER IS: _____

MY LEAST FAVOURITE TEACHER IS:_____

IN MY SCHOOL THERE ARE _____PUPILS.

IN MY CLASS THERE ARE_____PUPILS.

THIS IS WHAT MY SCHOOL LOOKS LIKE:

(Do a drawing of your school.)

THESE ARE THE NAMES AND AGES OF THE OTHER PEOPLE IN MY CLASS:
(Give each pupil a mark out of 10. The people you like most will get high marks. The people you don't like will get low marks.)

NAME   NICKNAME   AGE   MARK OUT OF 10

THE SUBJECT I AM BEST AT IS: _____

THE SUBJECT I AM WORST AT IS: _____

THE SUBJECT I LIKE BEST IS: _____

THE SUBJECT I LIKE LEAST IS: _____

THE BEST MEAL WE GET AT SCHOOL IS:_____

THE WORST MEAL WE GET AT SCHOOL IS: _____

I BELONG TO THESE SCHOOL SOCIETIES/CLUBS:

1. _____

2. _____

3. _____

4. _____

MY SCHOOL UNIFORM LOOKS LIKE THIS:

(Do a drawing of your school uniform.)

I LIKE MY SCHOOL UNIFORM: _____(Yes or No)

MY SCHOOL COLOURS ARE: _____

MY SCHOOL MOTTO IS: _____

MY OTHER SCHOOLS HAVE BEEN:

Name of school   Dates when I was there

1. _____

2. _____

3. _____

I HOPE MY NEXT SCHOOL WILL BE: _____

_____

I HOPE I WILL GO TO COLLEGE/UNIVERSITY_____
                                      (Yes or No)

I HAVE BEEN GOING TO SCHOOL FOR _____YEARS.
(Count the number of years you have been going
to school.)

I HAVE BEEN GOING TO SCHOOL FOR _____TERMS.
(Count the number of terms you have spent at
school.)

I HAVE SPENT_____DAYS AT SCHOOL IN MY LIFE
SO FAR.
(Work out how many days there are in each term
and add up the number of days you have spent
at school in your life so far.)

50

I HAVE SPENT_____HOURS AT SCHOOL IN MY LIFE SO FAR.
(If you have worked out how many days you have spent at school, you can now work out exactly the number of hours you have spent at school as well!)

THESE ARE THE SPORTS I PLAY:

(List all the sports you ever play here. Give yourself a mark out of 10 for how good you are at each sport and another mark out of 10 for how much enjoyment you get out of a sport. For example, if you love netball but are not a very good netball player, give yourself 10 out of 10 for enjoyment, but only 5 out of 10 for skill.)

NAME OF SPORT	ENJOYMENT SCORE	SKILL SCORE

THIS IS A SPORT I'D LIKE TO TRY: _____
(If there is a sport you've never tried but would like to one day – it can be anything from boxing and fencing to hang-gliding and rowing – put it here.)

THE FASTEST TIME IN WHICH I CAN RUN 100 METRES IS:
_____
(You might like to know that the world record is 9.95 secs.)

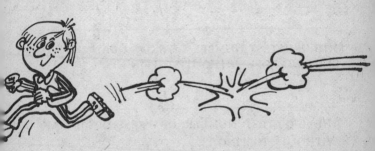

THE FASTEST TIME IN WHICH I CAN RUN 1,000 METRES IS:
_____
(The world record is 2 mins. 13.9 secs.)

THE FASTEST TIME IN WHICH I CAN RUN 1 MILE IS:

_____
(The world record is 3 mins. 48.95 secs.)

THE HIGHEST I CAN JUMP IS: _____
(The world record is 7 ft. 8½ ins.)

THE FURTHEST I CAN JUMP IS: _____
(The world record is 29 ft. 2½ ins.)

THE LONGEST I CAN KEEP RUNNING ON THE SPOT IS:

_____

(There's no world record for this, so you can make your own!)

THE GREATEST NUMBER OF HOPS ON THE SAME FOOT
THAT I CAN DO WITHOUT STOPPING IS:

_____

THE GREATEST NUMBER OF SKIPS I CAN DO WITH A
SKIPPING ROPE WITHOUT STOPPING IS:

_____

THE GREATEST NUMBER OF PRESS-UPS I CAN DO
WITHOUT STOPPING IS:

_____

MY FAVOURITE SPORT TO WATCH IS: _____

THE SPORT I LEAST LIKE WATCHING IS: _____

MY FAVOURITE FOOTBALL TEAM IS: _____

MY FAVOURITE SPORTSMAN IS: _____

MY FAVOURITE SPORTSWOMAN IS: _____
54

MY HOBBIES

MY HOBBIES ARE:

_____

_____

_____

THE HOBBY I WOULD MOST LIKE TO TRY IS:

_____

(Put an activity or pastime you've never tried but
would like to – it can be anything from stamp-
collecting and making model railways to magic
and bird-watching.)

MY FAVOURITE BOARD GAMES ARE:

_____

_____

_____

55

_____

_____

MY FAVOURITE PARTY GAMES ARE:

_____

_____

_____

_____

_____

MY TELEVISION

MY FAVOURITE TV PROGRAMME IS: _____

THE PROGRAMME I HATE MOST IS: _____

I THINK THESE ARE THE BEST AND WORST PRO-
GRAMMES ON TV:

	THE BEST	THE WORST
Children's programme:	_____	

_____

News programme: _____

_____

Science programme:_____

_____

Quiz show:_____

Cartoon film:_____

Adventure film: _____

Drama series: _____

Comedy series: _____

Musical programme: _____

Commercial: _____

MY FAVOURITE MALE TV STAR IS:_____

MY FAVOURITE FEMALE TV STAR IS: _____

THE LATEST I HAVE EVER STAYED UP WATCHING TV IS:

_____

Pop music

MY FAVOURITE MALE SINGER IS: _____

MY FAVOURITE FEMALE SINGER IS:_____

MY FAVOURITE BAND IS:_____

I THINK THE BEST SINGLE EVER RECORDED IS: _____

_____

I THINK THE BEST ALBUM EVER RECORDED IS: _____

_____

MY FAVOURITE DISC JOCKEY IS: _____

_____

IF I COULD BE A MEMBER OF ANY ROCK BAND IN THE WORLD, I WOULD WANT TO BE A MEMBER OF THIS ONE:

_____

Classical music

MY FAVOURITE COMPOSER IS: _____

MY FAVOURITE PIECE OF MUSIC IS:_____

MY FAVOURITE BALLET IS: _____

MY FAVOURITE OPERA IS: _____

MY FAVOURITE ORCHESTRAL INSTRUMENT IS: _____

_____

IF I COULD BE A MEMBER OF A SYMPHONY ORCHESTRA,
I WOULD WANT TO PLAY:

_____

(If you don't want to play an instrument, you can
choose to be the conductor instead.)

I AM LEARNING TO PLAY THIS MUSICAL INSTRU-
MENT:

_____

MY SCORE IS:_____

(Give yourself a mark out of 10 for how good you
are. If you play the violin and your name is
Yehudi Menuhin give yourself 10. If you had
your first lesson today and broke the bow and all
four of the strings give yourself 1!)

I WOULD LIKE TO LEARN TO PLAY THIS MUSICAL
INSTRUMENT:

_____

MY SIGNATURE

If you asked a famous author for his autograph and he wrote 'Squashed Tomato', you would think he was trying to be funny. In fact, though, an autograph doesn't have to be somebody's name: it just has to be an example of their *handwriting*. When you ask someone to give you their autograph, you are only asking for a sample of their handwriting. If you want them to sign their name for you, you should ask for their signature. Write your signature here.

Right hand:

Left hand:

Here is the timetable of my day:
(Make a note of what you are doing during every hour of the day. Your day will be different during the term time from what it is during the holidays and Saturday and Sunday will be different from weekdays.)

TIME	MONDAY/FRIDAY IN TERM TIME	MONDAY/FRIDAY DURING THE HOLIDAYS
0600 Hours		
0700		
0800		
0900		
1000		

62

1100

1200

1300

1400

1500

1600

1700

1800

1900

2000

2100

2200

TIME	SATURDAY	SUNDAY

0600 Hours

0700

0800

0900

1000

1100

1200

1300

1400

1500

1600

1700

1800

1900

2000

MY BEDTIME IS AT _____ON MONDAYS

_____ON TUESDAYS

_____ON WEDNESDAYS

_____ON THURSDAYS

_____ON FRIDAYS

_____ON SATURDAYS

_____ON SUNDAYS

THE LATEST I HAVE EVER STAYED UP UNTIL IS: ____

_____ 11.30 _____

(The average length of a night's sleep among adults is 7 hours and 36 minutes. Children sleep longer. How many hours of sleep do you have in a week? Use this sleep chart to work out how much sleep you get in a week. Every morning mark the number of hours you slept the night before.)

66

MY SLEEP CHART:

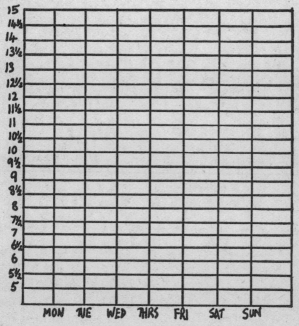

THE NICEST DREAM I HAVE EVER HAD:

(You can either describe the dream in words or try to draw a picture of it here.)

THE WORST NIGHTMARE I HAVE EVER HAD:

(You can either describe the nightmare in words or try to draw a picture of it here.)

MY FOOD

IF I COULD HAVE ANY MEAL AT ALL, THIS IS WHAT I
WOULD CHOOSE TO HAVE:

_____

THE FOOD I LIKE LEAST OF ALL IS:

_____

MY FAVOURITE DRINK IS:

_____

MY LEAST FAVOURITE DRINK IS:

_____

MY FAVOURITE BREAKFAST CEREAL IS:

_____

MY LEAST FAVOURITE BREAKFAST CEREAL IS:

_____

MY FAVOURITE KIND OF SPREAD IS:

_____

MY LEAST FAVOURITE KIND OF SPREAD IS:

_____

MY FAVOURITE KIND OF MEAT IS:

_____

MY LEAST FAVOURITE KIND OF MEAT IS:

_____

MY FAVOURITE VEGETABLE IS:

_____

MY LEAST FAVOURITE VEGETABLE IS:

_____

MY FAVOURITE FRUIT IS:

_____

MY LEAST FAVOURITE FRUIT IS:

_____

MY FAVOURITE PUDDING IS:

_____

MY LEAST FAVOURITE PUDDING IS:

_____

MY FAVOURITE ICE CREAM FLAVOUR IS:

_____

MY LEAST FAVOURITE ICE CREAM FLAVOUR IS:

_____

MY FAVOURITE SWEET IS:

_____

MY LEAST FAVOURITE SWEET IS:

_____

FOREIGN FOOD

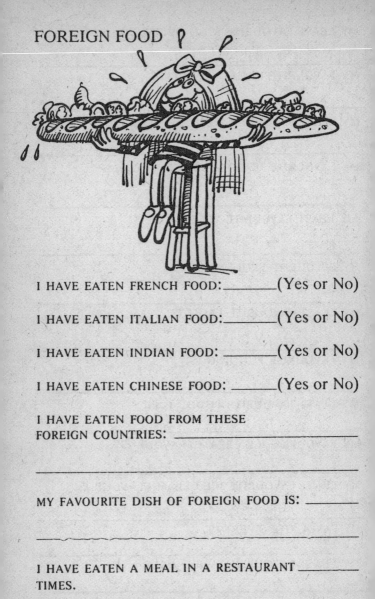

I HAVE EATEN FRENCH FOOD: _____ (Yes or No)

I HAVE EATEN ITALIAN FOOD: _____ (Yes or No)

I HAVE EATEN INDIAN FOOD: _____ (Yes or No)

I HAVE EATEN CHINESE FOOD: _____ (Yes or No)

I HAVE EATEN FOOD FROM THESE
FOREIGN COUNTRIES: _____

_____

MY FAVOURITE DISH OF FOREIGN FOOD IS: _____

_____

I HAVE EATEN A MEAL IN A RESTAURANT _____
TIMES.

MY CLOTHES

AROUND THE NECK I MEASURE: _____

AROUND THE CHEST I MEASURE: _____

AROUND THE WAIST I MEASURE: _____

AROUND THE HIPS I MEASURE: _____

I TAKE CLOTHES SIZE: _____

I WEAR SHOES SIZE: _____

OF ALL MY CLOTHES THESE ARE THE ONES I LIKE

WEARING MOST: _____

_____

_____

_____

OF ALL MY CLOTHES THESE ARE THE ONES I LIKE

WEARING LEAST: _____

_____

_____

_____

74

IF I COULD DESIGN MY OWN CLOTHES, THIS IS WHAT THEY WOULD LOOK LIKE:

IF OUR ILLUSTRATOR COULD
DESIGN HIS OWN CLOTHES,
THIS IS WHAT THEY WOULD
LOOK LIKE:

MY PRESENTS

HERE IS A LIST OF THE BEST PRESENTS I HAVE BEEN GIVEN:

_____

_____

_____

_____

_____

_____

MY BOOKS

I HAVE GOT _____ BOOKS.

THESE ARE MY TEN FAVOURITE BOOKS.
(As well as giving the title and author of the
books, mark each one out of 10. If the book you
like best of all is this one give it 10 out of 10!)

TITLE	AUTHOR	SCORE

1.

2.

3.

4.

5.

6.

7.

8.

9.

10.

80

THESE ARE THE BOOKS I HAVEN'T YET READ BUT THAT I MOST WANT TO READ:

1. _____

2. _____

3. _____

4. _____

5. _____

6. _____

IF I WROTE A STORY THIS IS WHAT I WOULD CALL IT:

_____

(Give the title of your book here.)

THIS IS THE NAME THAT I WOULD GIVE TO THE HERO/HEROINE OF MY STORY:

_____

IF I WROTE A BOOK THAT WASN'T A STORY BOOK, THIS IS THE SUBJECT I WOULD MOST LIKE TO WRITE ABOUT:

_____

MY MONEY

THIS IS HOW MUCH MONEY I HAVE:

IN CASH: £   .   p

IN A PIGGY BANK: £   .   p

IN A SAVINGS BANK: £   .   p
   Account No._____

IN THE POST OFFICE: £   .   p
   Account No. _____

IN PREMIUM BONDS: £   .   p
   Bondholder's No. _____
   Bond Nos. _____

OTHER MONEY THAT I HAVE: £   .   p

WHERE IT IS: _____

THIS IS HOW MUCH POCKET MONEY I GET EACH WEEK:

50p

_____

MY TRANSPORT

MY FAMILY CAR IS A: _____

THE REGISTRATION NUMBER IS: _____

THE LICENCE IS DUE FOR RENEWAL IN: _____

THE OTHER VEHICLES BELONGING TO THE FAMILY ARE:
(Roller skates, skateboards, sledges and toy tricycles don't count. Only list vehicles that actually travel on the main road.)

_____ _____

_____

_____

EVERY DAY I GO TO SCHOOL BY: _____

MY IDEAL FAMILY CAR WOULD BE: _____

IN MY LIFE I HAVE TRAVELLED IN OR ON:
(Please tick)

CAR	POGO STICK
VAN	UNICYCLE
LORRY	BICYCLE
CARAVAN	TRICYCLE
COACH	INVALID CARRIAGE
BUS	AMBULANCE
DOUBLE-DECKER BUS	TANDEM
UNDERGROUND	MOTORBIKE
LIFT	SCOOTER
ESCALATOR	GLIDER

84

MOVING PAVEMENT	PROPELLOR AEROPLANE
CANOE	JET AEROPLANE
SAILING BOAT	CONCORDE
STEAM SHIP	BALLOON
OCEAN LINER	HORSE
CATAMARAN	DONKEY
WATER SKIS	HORSE-DRAWN CARRIAGE
HOVERCRAFT	ELEPHANT
HYDROFOIL	CAMEL

Other means of transport I have used:

_____

_____

OF ALL THE PEOPLE I HAVE MET AND KNOW THIS IS
THE MAN I ADMIRE MOST:

Name:

Address:

Age:

Occupation:

(Put a picture or drawing of the person here.)

OF ALL THE PEOPLE I HAVE MET AND KNOW THIS IS
THE WOMAN I ADMIRE MOST:

Name:

Address:

Age:

Occupation:

(Put a picture or drawing of the person here.)

OF ALL THE FAMOUS PEOPLE ALIVE IN THE WORLD
TODAY, THIS IS THE MAN I ADMIRE MOST:

Name:

Age:

Occupation:

(Put a picture or drawing of the person here.)

OF ALL THE FAMOUS PEOPLE ALIVE IN THE WORLD
TODAY, THIS IS THE WOMAN I ADMIRE MOST:

Name:

Age:

Occupation:

(Put a picture or drawing of the person here.)

OF ALL THE GREAT FIGURES OF HISTORY, THIS IS THE
PERSON I ADMIRE MOST:

Name:

When they lived:

Occupation:

(Put a picture or drawing of the person here.)

OF ALL THE CHARACTERS WHO NEVER LIVED BUT WHO HAVE BEEN MADE FAMOUS IN NOVELS OR PLAYS OR IN FILMS OR ON TELEVISION, THIS IS THE PERSON I ADMIRE MOST:

Name:

(Put a picture or drawing of the person here.)

MY SENSE OF HUMOUR

MY FAVOURITE JOKE OR RIDDLE_____

_____

_____

_____

_____

_____

_____

_____

_____

MY FAVOURITE COMEDIAN IS:_____

MY FAVOURITE TV COMEDY PROGRAMME IS:_____

MY FAVOURITE CARTOON CHARACTER IS: _____

MY FAVOURITE CARTOON STRIP IS: _____

MY FAVOURITE NEWSPAPER CARTOONIST IS: _____

MY FUNNIEST FRIEND IS: _____

THIS IS WHAT MAKES ME LOSE MY TEMPER MOST:

_____

_____

_____

_____

_____

_____

_____

MY LIKES AND DISLIKES

	MY FAVOURITE IS	MY LEAST FAVOURITE IS
Colour	Black	
Number	5	
Day of the Week	Wensday	
Month	Augest	January
Smell	~~pasyn~~	petrol
Country	AMarica	China
Town		

96

Painting

Fabric

Metal

Jewel

Flavour

Time of day

Noise

Person

MY DAYDREAMS

IF I COULD BE ANYONE I KNOW RATHER THAN BEING WHO I AM, THIS IS WHO I WOULD BE:

Terry Wogan

IF I COULD BE ANYONE FAMOUS WHO IS LIVING IN THE WORLD TODAY, THIS IS WHO I WOULD BE:

IF I COULD BE ANYONE FROM HISTORY, THIS IS WHO I WOULD BE:

IF I COULD BE ANYONE FROM FICTION, THIS IS WHO I WOULD BE:

IF I HAD A MILLION POUNDS, THIS IS HOW I WOULD SPEND IT:

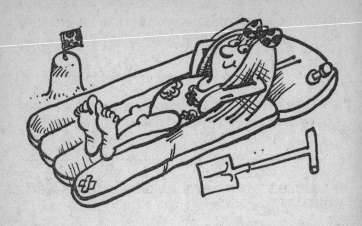

IF I COULD DO ANYTHING AT ALL TOMORROW, THIS IS WHAT I WOULD DO:

_____

_____

_____

_____

_____

_____

_____

MY FUTURE

WHEN I GROW UP WHAT WILL MY JOB BE?

MY GUESS IS:_____

WHEN I GROW UP WHERE WILL I LIVE?

MY GUESS IS:_____

WILL I BE RICH?

MY GUESS IS:_____

WILL I BE FAMOUS?

MY GUESS IS:_____

WILL I MAKE AN IMPORTANT DISCOVERY?

MY GUESS IS:_____

WILL I TRAVEL THE WORLD?

MY GUESS IS:_____

101

HOW OLD WILL I LIVE TO BE?

MY GUESS IS:_____

WILL I GET MARRIED?

MY GUESS IS:_____

WHEN WILL I GET MARRIED?

MY GUESS IS:_____

WHO WILL I MARRY?

MY GUESS IS:_____

HOW MANY CHILDREN WILL I HAVE?

MY GUESS IS:_____

WHAT NAMES WILL THEY HAVE?

     THE BOYS   THE GIRLS

(Be sure you never throw away or lose your copy of *ME!* In twenty years' time you must look at it again and see how many of your guesses turned out to be correct ones.)

HERE ARE SOME MORE KNIGHT BOOKS.
TICK THE ONES YOU HAVE READ.

AMAZON ADVENTURE by Willard Price
Have you read any of the other thirteen books in this series?

FIVE ON A TREASURE ISLAND by Enid Blyton
What other stories have you read about the Famous Five?

BLACK BEAUTY by Anna Sewell

PETER PAN AND WENDY by J. M. Barrie

Have you heard of SNOOPY? BIGGLES? ASTERIX? THE BLACK STALLION? They are all in Knight Books.